A NOTE TO PARENTS ABOUT COMPLAINING

If it is true that our thoughts contribute greatly to the creation of our reality, excessive or unjustifiable complaining can be extremely counterproductive. Negative comments seldom help make things better. Indeed, they usually make things worse.

This is not to say that one should not address wrongs that need to be made right. The purpose of this book is to teach children when it is appropriate to complain and when it is not. In addition, this book encourages children to be positive as much as possible and to utilize negative responses only when absolutely necessary.

By discussing this book with your child, you can reduce the complaining that often aggravates difficult family situations. This will go a long way toward creating a happier and healthier home environment.

Complaining is often a learned behavior. Many children learn to complain by watching their parents complain. If you are committed to keeping your child's complaints to a minimum, it is important that you minimize the amount you complain. It is always far more productive and satisfying to determine that "your glass is half full instead of half empty."

This book belongs to:

Eric

ɔịnɔ̃

© 2005 Joy Berry. All rights reserved.

No part of this publication may be reproduced in whole or in part, or stored in
a retrieval system, or transmitted in any form or by any means, electronic, mechanical,
photocopying, recording, or otherwise, without written permission of the publisher.
For information regarding permission, write to: Scholastic Inc.,
Attention: Permissions Department, 557 Broadway, New York, NY 10012.

Published by Scholastic Inc.
90 Old Sherman Turnpike, Danbury, CT 06816.

SCHOLASTIC and associated logos are trademarks and/or
registered trademarks of Scholastic Inc.

ISBN 0-7172-8595-2

First Scholastic Printing, October 2005

A Book About
Complaining

by
Joy Berry

SCHOLASTIC INC.

New York   Toronto   London   Auckland   Sydney
Mexico City   New Delhi   Hong Kong   Buenos Aires

This book is about Amy and her friend Tami.

Reading about Amy and Tami can help you understand and deal with **complaining.**

You are complaining when you are not pleased with something and say so.

Complaining is saying that something is wrong. It is finding fault with something.

When you are with someone who keeps complaining:
- How do you feel?
- What do you think?
- What do you do?

When you are with someone who complains:
- You might feel unhappy and disappointed.
- You might think it is not fun to spend time with the person.
- You might decide you do not want to be around the person.

It is important to treat others the way you want to be treated.

If you do not want the people you are with to complain, you must not complain.

Too much complaining can make you feel bad.

It can cause you to think about the bad things around you instead of the good things.

Thinking about the bad things around you
can put you in a bad mood.

When you are in a bad mood:
- You will probably have a bad day.
- You might say or do things that hurt you or the people and things around you.

Complaining can be harmful to you and others.

This does not mean you should keep quiet when something is really wrong. Sometimes you might need to complain.

Think before you complain. Complain only if it will help change something that needs to be changed.

Accept things as they are if they cannot be changed. Do not continue to complain.

When you need to complain:
- Do it in a nice way.
- Try not to shout.
- Try not to throw a tantrum.

When you must complain, try to suggest ways to solve the problem.

Once you are sure your complaint is understood, stop complaining.

Listen to what others have to say. If they suggest a good solution to the problem, follow it.

Remember to think about the good things around you. Talk about them.

Do not complain unless you need to.

It is important to treat people the way you want to be treated.

If you do not want others to complain around you, you must not complain around them.